Margaret Elizabeth Munson Sangster

Easter Bells

Poems

Margaret Elizabeth Munson Sangster

Easter Bells
Poems

ISBN/EAN: 9783744709521

Printed in Europe, USA, Canada, Australia, Japan

Cover: Foto ©Thomas Meinert / pixelio.de

More available books at **www.hansebooks.com**

EASTER BELLS

Poems

BY

MARGARET E. SANGSTER

ILLUSTRATED

NEW YORK
HARPER AND BROTHERS
MDCCCXCVII

By MRS. SANGSTER.

WITH MY NEIGHBORS. 16mo, Cloth, Ornamental, $1 25.

ON THE ROAD HOME. Poems. Illustrated. 16mo, Cloth, Ornamental, $1 25.

LITTLE KNIGHTS AND LADIES. Poems. Illustrated. 16mo, Cloth, Ornamental, $1 25.

HOME FAIRIES AND HEART FLOWERS. Illustrated. 4to, Cloth, Ornamental, $6 00.

PUBLISHED BY HARPER & BROTHERS, NEW YORK.

Copyright, 1897, by HARPER & BROTHERS.

All rights reserved.

TO
MY DEAR FRIEND
CORNELIA REMSEN JOHNSON
THESE SIMPLE VERSES
Are Lovingly Inscribed

The poems here gathered, originally appeared in the several publications of Messrs. HARPER & BROTHERS, or in *The Cosmopolitan Magazine, The Youth's Companion, The Congregationalist, The Christian Intelligencer,* and *The Sunday-School Times.*

CONTENTS

Part I—SONGS OF THE EASTER-TIDE

	Page
EASTER BELLS	3
AWAKENING	4
GETHSEMANE	5
GOOD-FRIDAY	7
AN EASTER SONG	9
"WHO ROSE AGAIN FROM THE DEAD"	11
THE SPLENDOR OF LILIES	14
EASTER CHORDS	15
UNDER THE CLOUD	18
ANGELS	20
WHEN SPRING COMES BACK	22
AN EASTER IDYL	24
IN THE SHADOW	28
A DREAM	30
A WAY-SIDE GRAVE	31

	Page
COMFORT ONE ANOTHER	33
GOD'S WAY	35
EASTER FLOWERS	37

Part II—HOME AND HEARTH

LOVE'S KINGDOM	41
WHEN POLLY PLAYED FOR DANCING	42
WEDDED HANDS	44
THE AMBULANCE	45
THE HOME-BOUND SHIP	46
A COQUETTE	47
CAMP ECHOES	48
THE REASON	50
THREE BASKETS	51
CONVALESCENT	53
HER LETTER	54
BON VOYAGE!	56
SNOWDROP AND CROCUS	58
VIOLETS	59
A CLUSTER OF ROSES TO A FRIEND	60
THE BLOOM OF THE CACTUS	62
INFELIX	64
DAY BY DAY	66
THE OLD SCHOOL-HOUSE	68

	Page
THE MOTHER'S CHAIR	71
THE LETTER SHE DID NOT WRITE	73
THE UNRETURNING	75
THANKSGIVING	77

Part III—Mile-Stones

CHRISTMAS	81
AUTUMN PLOUGHING	83
THE CHRISTMAS ANGELS	85
HOLLY AND PINE	87
MISS LUCINDA'S OPINION	89
OF ALL DEAR DAYS	92
IN BETHLEHEM	95
A CHRISTMAS THOUGHT	97
OCTOBER	99
A THANKSGIVING FEAST	100
GARDENS	103
AUTUMN DAYS	105
THE LOVING-CUP	107
THE DAYS WHEN NOTHING HAPPENS	110
GOOD-NIGHT	112
THE NEW YEAR	114
AT THE PARTING OF THE WAYS	116
THE THINNING RANKS	118

Part IV—CLOSET AND ALTAR

	Page
JESUS WENT BEFORE	123
NOT READY	124
JOINT HEIRS	125
THE DEAREST ONE	127
A SONG OF THE BURDEN BEARER	129
VESPERS	131
ONE STEP AT A TIME	133
THE WORD SHE REMEMBERED	136
TE DEUM LAUDAMUS	137
THINE IS THE POWER	139
A THOUGHT	140
FOLDED HANDS	141
THE CURTAIN FALLS	143

ILLUSTRATIONS

"NEVER YET WAS A SPRING-TIME WHEN
    THE BUDS FORGOT TO BLOW" *Frontispiece*

MAIDEN BERTHA . . . . . *Facing p.* 52

"THE DEAR OLD GARDENS . . . WHERE
    MOTHER USED TO POTTER ABOUT"
                              Facing p. 104

"IN THE FIELDS ARE SILENCE AND
    PERFUME" . . . . . . *Facing p.* 132

Part 1

SONGS OF THE EASTER-TIDE

EASTER BELLS

Chime, solemn bells of Easter!
  The shadows flee away,
And all the earth is smiling
  In the glory of the day.

Ring, tender bells of Easter!
  Beyond our toil and tears,
There wait for all the faithful
  Heaven's long and happy years.

Break, joyous bells of Easter!
  From far across the sea
Bring us the endless music
  Of immortality.

Triumphant bells of Easter!
  Again by angels rung,
Speak comfort to the sorrowing
  Of every land and tongue.

Blend, golden bells of Easter!
   Heaven's fairest and its best,
To hush earth's clamorous discords
   And soothe earth's sad unrest.

AWAKENING

Never yet was a spring-time,
   Late though lingered the snow,
That the sap stirred not at the whisper
   Of the south wind, sweet and low;
Never yet was a spring-time
   When the buds forgot to blow.

Ever the wings of the summer
   Are folded under the mould;
Life, that has known no dying,
   Is Love's, to have and to hold,
Till sudden, the bourgeoning Easter!
   The song! the green and the gold!

GETHSEMANE

The dew lay thick on thorn and flower,
   And where the olives clustered gray
Weird shapes, within that awesome hour
   Between the midnight and the day,
Seemed walking phantom-like abroad,
As if to vex the Son of God.

And all the city lay asleep,
   O'er beast and bird the spell was cast,
And nothing stirred the silence deep,
   Save where our Lord the vigil passed;
The long lone vigil when His prayer
Was uttered from a heart's despair.

"Oh, watch with me one little hour!"
   His tender tones had pleading cried
Unto the faithful three, whose dower
   Of love had kept them near His side.
Nay—folded hands and drooping head,
And slumber—quiet as the dead.

No wonder then for weariness
   The second time they fall asleep,
He turns in very tenderness,
   And leaves them to repose so deep;
Alone He meets the serpent foe,
Alone He bears the bitter woe.

Gethsemane! Gethsemane!
   We see the glory and the gloom!
Through all thy pain and agony,
   Thy garden wears immortal bloom.
'Twas human friendship failed Him there,
But Love Divine did hear His prayer.

Life's bitter cups we too must take,
   Life's bitter bread in anguish eat;
But when our hearts are like to break
   There comes to us a whisper sweet,
"Fear thou no dim Gethsemane;
Thy sleepless Friend will watch with thee!"

GOOD-FRIDAY

Be hushed, my heart, remembering
   What dole was given for thee,
How pressed on Him thy burden, when,
For all the sinful sons of men,
   Christ went to Calvary.

The mournful journey that He made,
   Each step was taken for thee.
Be hushed, my heart, let clamor cease;
Prepare a chamber white with peace,
   His resting-place to be.

In solemn shadow of the cross,
   O soul, abide till He
Who tasted death ere thou shouldst know
Its bitterness of utmost woe
   With strength shall guerdon thee.

Its Via Dolorosa still
    Each life of earth must see,
And in some hour, or soon or late,
Must bend beneath the crushing weight
    Of earth's Gethsemane.

But heart, in love and prayer look up
    Beyond the awesome tree;
The heaven of heavens is reft to-day;
All angels march the starry way
    That leads from Calvary.

For conquering, the Lord of life
    (His mighty legions free)
Goes forward while the ages roll;
The price of every ransomed soul
    Full paid on Calvary.

AN EASTER SONG

The golden sun climbs up the sky,
    The shadows flee away,
Oh! weary heart, forget to sigh,
    God sends thee Easter Day!
Long was the night, chill was the air,
    And grief o'er brooded long,
Yet is the new world white and fair,
    Uplift thine Easter song!

The cross that bowed thee with its weight
    By strength of prayer is stirred,
Till it shall bear thee soon or late,
    As wings upbear the bird.
The life that thrills from star to star,
    And beats in leaf and stem,
Is wider than the heavens are,
    And blesses thee from them.

Wert thou cast down, wert thou dismayed,
    Dear child of One above,
Behold the earth in light arrayed,
    The light of deathless love.

Oh! listen to the word that wakes
  In every budding flower,
And take the bread the Master breaks,
  In His triumphant hour.

Nor feel, dear one whom Jesus saves,
  And heartens day by day,
That earth is but a place of graves,
  A dim and dolorous way.
As mothers hush their little ones,
  God puts his own to sleep;
And long as time is marked by suns,
Their beds His angels keep.

Not once a year alone, but oft
  In all our years of days,
Shall fall the word or promise, soft
  As hymns the blessed raise.
If but we bend the listening ear
  To hear upon the strand
The wave-beat of the endless life,
  Not far, but close at hand.

For those who hear, and hearing yearn,
  The King hath secrets sweet;
Their hearts within them thrill and burn,
  They wait His coming feet.

Then swift the sun climbs up the sky!
  The shadows flee away!
Oh! weary heart, forget to sigh,
  God sends thee Easter Day!

"WHO ROSE AGAIN FROM THE DEAD"

O Earth, forget thy winter; O Nature, bud
    and bloom,
And clothe the slopes with greenness that
    late were hung with gloom.
O clustered Easter lilies, your gleaming cen-
    sers lift,
Forth comes the mighty Victor, the rocky
    tomb to rift.

O gentle Easter angels, be swift to greet the
    day
When from the guarded chamber the stone
    is rolled away,
And Christ the King steps onward, with
    Death beneath him dead,
And leads His ransomed homeward, with
    glory on His head.

THE SPLENDOR OF LILIES

Oh, rare as the splendor of lilies,
   And sweet as the violet's breath,
Comes the jubilant morning of Easter,
   The triumph of life over death;
And fresh from the earth's quickened bosom
   Full baskets of flowers we bring,
And scatter their satin soft petals
   To carpet a path for our King.

In the countless green blades of the meadow,
   The sheen of the daffodil's gold,
In the tremulous blue on the mountains,
   The opaline mist on the wold,
In the tinkle of brooks through the pasture,
   The river's strong sweep to the sea,
Are signs of the day that is hasting
   In gladness to you and to me.

Oh, dawn in thy splendor of lilies,
   Thy fluttering violet breath,
Oh, jubilant morning of Easter,
   Thou triumph of life over death!
Then fresh from the earth's quickened bosom
   Full baskets of flowers we bring,
And scatter their satin soft petals
   To carpet a path for our King.

EASTER CHORDS

CHRIST the Lord is risen to-day!
Sons of men and angels say,
Raise your joys and triumphs high,
Sing ye heavens, and earth reply.

Sweet, sweet and clear the dear old strain
    across the aisles is pealing,
The choir uplifts its stately chords that
    throb with tender feeling,
For never time as Easter time brings gladness to our eyes,
When morning unto evening tells the rapture of the skies.

Love's redeeming work is done,
Fought the fight, the battle's won.
Lo! the sun's eclipse is o'er,
Lo! He sets in blood no more.

Again we read the wondrous tale, how on
    the Cross they bound Him,
How Jew and Roman jeered and scoffed in
    cruel throngs around Him,

Till noon forgot its light in gloom and all the world grew black,
While He who came to save us paid the price with naught held back.

Vain the stone, the watch, the seal;
Christ hath burst the gates of hell!
Death in vain forbids His rise,
Christ hath opened Paradise.

Oh! listen, thrilling far and loud the Gloria strains excelling,
For death for evermore is dead, triumphant shouts are swelling.
They who have passed beyond the stream and reached the other side,
Exult in life that never ends; with Christ are satisfied.

Hail, the Lord of earth and heaven!
Praise to Thee by both be given!
Thee we greet triumphant now;
Hail! the Resurrection Thou!

In solemn joy, in trustful hope, in faith that cannot falter,
This Easter Day we bring our meed of praises to God's altar.

All crowns are set on Christ's dear head,
   the crown of thorns that wore;
Forever and forever more our Saviour we
   adore.

Oh! risen Lord victorious, oh! Son of God
   Most High,
Who for our sins did bear the yoke, who
   came for us to die;
In Thee we conquer death and hell, in Thee
   we rise and reign;
Life throbs to-day victorious in every pulsing
   vein.

We have no fear, we have no doubt, we read
   redemption's story,
And earth and heaven together meet in
   ecstasies of glory.

UNDER THE CLOUD

Under the cloud we pass,
  The cloud that dims our skies,
  The hot tears blur our eyes,
We enter the cloud, alas!

We mourn for our darling gone;
  For the days that come no more,
  With her laugh at the dear home door;
We are desolate, being alone.

We sigh for the might-have-beens,
  For the words we did not say—
  Was it only yesterday?—
And memory sits and spins

A web that is like a shroud,
  So thick and dark does it fold,
  Woe for the tale that is told!
Like children we cry aloud.

For when she was here, and yet
   Our own, for love's sweet grace,
   When the lighting up of her face
Could banish our dull regret

And give us surcease from pain,
   We took as a common thing
   (Ah! there is the sharpened sting)
The touch, the look, the strain,

The music and cheer she gave—
   And now she is gone away,
   Lost into heaven's bright day;
And we—plant flowers on her grave.

Aye, friends, we are under the cloud,
   So white, and chill, and thick,
   And the heart grows faint and sick,
So fast do our wan thoughts crowd.

But the cloud has an upper side,
   And somewhere out of the blue
   Our darling is looking through,
And our sorrow is glorified.

ANGELS

In the old days God sent His angels oft
   To men in threshing-floors, to women pressed
With daily tasks; they came to tent and croft,
   And whispered words of blessing and of rest.

Not mine to guess what shape those angels wore,
   Nor tell what voice they spoke, nor with what grace
They brought the dear love down that evermore
   Makes lowliest souls its best abiding place.

But in these days I know my angels well;
   They brush my garments on the common way,
They take my hand, and very softly tell
   Some bit of comfort in the waning day.

And though their angel-names I do not ken,
  Though in their faces human love I read,
They are God-given to this world of men,
  God-sent to bless it in its hours of need.

Child, mother, dearest wife, brave hearts that take
  The rough and bitter cross, and help us bear
Its heavy weight when strength is like to break,
  God bless you all, our angels unaware!

WHEN SPRING COMES BACK

When Spring comes back the violets lift
   Their shyly hooded faces,
Where late the frozen snows adrift
   Heaped high the woodland spaces.
When Spring comes back the sunbeams dance
   On green leaves all a-quiver,
And grasses rally, spear and lance,
   By rippling brook and river.

When Spring comes back the lilies haste,
   What time the bells are ringing,
To bring their perfumes, pure and chaste,
   From hallowed censers swinging.
Shine dim church aisles on Easter day
   Beneath the lilied whiteness,
And happy children kneel and pray
   Amid the serried brightness.

When Spring comes back a merry train,
   Of merry wings come with her,
The robin and the wren again
   Come gayly flitting hither;

The bluebird and the oriole,
  The martin and the swallow.
"Away," they chant, "with grief and dole,
  Here's spring, and summer 'll follow!"

When Spring comes back, when Spring comes
      back,
  Chill winter will be over!
Erelong we'll hear the elfin drums
  Where bees are deep in clover.
After we catch the swaying lilt
  Of winds among the daisies,
And see the rose-cups' sweetness spilt
  Among the garden mazes.

AN EASTER IDYL

MANY a year the Easter came, laughing o'er
    land and sea,
   Wafting the perfume of lilies wherever its
     dawn-light fell,
Kindling the flames of the roses, and waving
    their torches free,
   Far over hill and mountain, and deep in
     the lonesome dell.

And many a year at Easter I sat in the old
    church loft,
   And lifted my voice in Te Deums, and
     sang like a mavis clear,
Sang of glory and triumph, and my voice
    thrilled sweet and soft,
   O! many a time in the Easter of many a
     cloudless year.

Till there fell a season of anguish, when the
    stars went out in the sky,
   When I covered my face, and bent my
     knees, and beat with a hopeless prayer

At the golden gates of heaven that were
    shut to my bitter cry,
  While the Angel of Death at my threshold
    was deaf to my love's despair.

Then, straight on that wild, bleak winter
    there followed the fairest spring,
  With snowdrops and apple blossoms in
    riotous haste to bloom,
With the sudden note of the robin, and the
    flash of the bluebird's wing ;—
  And all that was mine of its beauty was
    the turf that covered a tomb.

O! the bells rang out for Easter, rang strong
    and sweet and shrill,
  And the organ's rolling thunder pealed
    through the long church aisle,
And the children fluttered with flowers, and
    I sat mute and still,
  I who had clean forgotten both how to
    pray and to smile.

And I murmured in fierce rebellion: "There
    is naught that endures below,
  Naught but the lamentations that are rent
    from souls in pain;"

And the joy of the Easter music, it struck
    on my ears like a blow,
  For I knew that my day was over, I could
    never be glad again!

And then—how it happened I know not—
    there was One in my sight who stood,
  And lo! on His brow was the thorn-print, in
    His hands were the nails' rough scars,
And the shadow that lay before Him was
    the shade of the holy rood,
  But the glow in His eyes was deeper than
    the light of the morning stars.

"Daughter," He said, "have comfort! Arise!
    keep Easter-tide!
  I, for thy sins who suffered and died on
    the cruel tree,
I, who was dead, am living; no evil shall e'er
    betide
  Those who, in earth or heaven, are pledged
    unto life with Me."

Now I wake to a holier Easter, happier than
    of old,
  And again my voice is lifted in Te Deums
    sweet and strong;

I send it to join the anthem in the wonderful
        city of gold,
   Where the hymns of the ransomed forever
        are timed to the Easter song.

And I can be glad with the gladness that is
        born of a perfect peace;
   On the strength of the Strong I am resting;
        I know that His will is best.
And who that has found that secret from
        darkness has won release,
   And even in sorrow's exile may lift up her
        eyes and be blessed.

IN THE SHADOW

We walk within the shadow, and we feel its thickening fold
That wraps us round and holds us close, a cloak against the cold;
The day is growing sombre, and the joyous light has fled,
And beneath our feet the road is rough, and clouds are overhead.

We sit within the shadow, and in that silence dumb,
To us in softened echoes remembered voices come;
Dear eyes that closed in slumber once, dear hands that straightened lie,
Awaken tender yearnings as the day wanes slowly by.

We rest within the shadow, though the hurrying people go
On errands swift for gold and gain, beyond us, to and fro;

We have no care for transient things ; we
    wish no more to strive
As once we did ; we rest, we dream, we feel
    but half alive.

Our resting and our waiting, and our plodding
    on the way,
With the sunshine of the past casting
    darkness on to-day,
With no caring for the future, while the
    heartache holds us fast,
With no thought for any pleasure—ah ! 'tis
    well these cannot last.

For the shadow always lifts, and the sunlight
    glows again ;
There are sudden gleams of brightness, sweet
    clear shining after rain ;
And we gird ourselves for action, strengthened
    we arise and go
From the sanctuary outward, where the feet
    tramp to and fro.

Life must have its sometime sorrow ; but
    the years that drift along
Touch the minor chords but seldom ; there
    are spaces blithe with song.

Sometimes we must face the shadow, where
    the wind blows keen and cold,
But the shadow fades at dawning, and the
    east is flecked with gold.

A DREAM

Some perfect day I shall not need
    To bend my brows o'er baffling tasks;
Some perfect day my eyes will read
    The meaning hid 'neath clouding masks;
Some perfect day my word and deed
    Will fill the ideal my spirit asks.

Dear perfect day of days to be,
    Which safe the steadfast heaven doth keep
Deep filled with love and rest for me,
    Close pressed with sheaves I yet shall reap,
When they who watch beside me see
    Only that I have fallen asleep.

A WAY-SIDE GRAVE

Our upland journey wound its way
Past hills that wore the green of May.

The dogwood starred the shadowy copse;
The light breeze rocked the pine-tree tops.

Far off we saw the village spires
And fluttering smoke of household fires.

But here of voice or tool no sound
Fell on the cloistered hush profound.

Sudden I drew my bridle rein,
Dim, shining out from moss and stain,

Alone amid a fallow field,
And half by brier and weed concealed,

I saw a rough stone cross that bore
One little dear home name; no more.

Some heart had ached, some house had known
The desolate hunger for its own,

When, hollowed out this narrow grave,
They laid, whom love had died to save

But could not, one whose name had been
To her own people "Josephine."

A ruined chimney, and the bloom
Of a pale purple lilac plume

Close by, and this small way-side cross
Told all the tale of love and loss;

While near and far the fragrant day
Was golden glimmering with May.

COMFORT ONE ANOTHER

Comfort one another;
   For the way is growing dreary,
   The feet are often weary,
And the heart is very sad.
   There is heavy burden-bearing,
   When it seems that none are caring,
And we half forget that ever we were glad.

Comfort one another
   With the hand-clasp close and tender,
   With the sweetness love can render,
And the look of friendly eyes.
   Do not wait with grace unspoken;
   While life's daily bread is broken,
Gentle speech is oft like manna from the skies.
   Comfort one another;
   There are words of music ringing
   Down the ages, sweet as singing

Of the happy choirs above.
    Ransomed saint and mighty angel
    Lift the grand, deep-voiced evangel,
Where forever they are praising the Eternal Love.

Comfort one another;
    By the hope of Him who sought us
    In our peril—Him who bought us,
Paying with His precious blood;
    By the faith that will not alter,
    Trusting strength that shall not falter,
Leaning on the One divinely good.

Comfort one another;
    Let the grave-gloom lie behind you,
    While the Spirit's words remind you
Of the home beyond the tomb,
    Where no more is pain or parting,
    Fever's flush or tear-drops starting,
But the presence of the Lord, and for all His people room.

GOD'S WAY

OUR way had been to smooth her upward
    road,
Easing the pressure of each heavy load,

Never to let her white hand know a soil,
Never her heart to feel the weight of toil,

Could we have shielded her from every care,
Kept her forever young and blithe and fair,

And from her body warded every pain,
As from her spirit all distress and strain,

This had been joy of joys, our chosen way.
God led her by a different path; each day

Sorrow and work and anxious care He gave,
And strife and anguish, till her soul grew
    brave.

Through weary nights she leaned upon His love,
Through cloudy days she fixed her gaze above.

Her dearest vanished, but in faith and trust
She knew them safe beyond the perished dust.

Refined by suffering, like a little child
She grew; into her Father's face she smiled.

And then, one day of days, an angel came;
In flute-notes sweet she heard him breathe her name.

Perhaps from out the rifted heaven she saw
Her mother's face look forth; in raptured awe

We caught the last swift glory in her eyes,
Ere, sleeping here, she woke in Paradise.

God's way was best, with reverent lips we say,
God's way *is* best, and praise our God to-day.

EASTER FLOWERS

Blooming to garland Easter,
   White as the drifted snows,
Are the beautiful vestal lilies,
   The myriad-petaled rose,
Carnations with hearts of fire,
   And the heather's fragrant spray—
Blooming to garland Easter,
   And strew our King's highway.

Late we had gloom and sorrow,
   But the word from Heaven forth
Has scattered the clouds before it
   Like a trumpet blown from the north;
And east and west and southward
   The flowers arise to-day
To garland the blithesome Easter,
   And strew the King's highway.

Carry the flowers of Easter
  To the darkened house of woe,
With their message of strength and comfort
  Let the lilies of Easter go;
Scatter the Easter blossoms
  In the little children's way;
Let want and pain and weakness
  Be cheered on our Easter day.

For lilac, and rose, and bluebell,
  And whatever name they wear,
The spell of the flowers of Easter
  Is a spell to banish care;
And blooming to garland Easter,
  They will shine in church to-day,
The lovely things that have awakened
  To deck our King's highway.

Part 11

HOME AND HEARTH

LOVE'S KINGDOM

You see no pomp of circumstance,
   No entourage of pride,
My lowly seeming to enhance
   As I walk by your side.
All day, at others' beck and call,
   My work obscure is done,
But off my shabby garments fall
     When comes the set of sun

You may not know it, friend, but then
   I, walking by your side,
Am crowned and sceptred, king of men.
   Let none my state deride;
For when I turn my own latch-key
   My wife is at the stair,
The baby claps her hands with glee,
   And I am royal there.

WHEN POLLY PLAYED FOR DANCING

When Polly played for dancing,
  Her slender fingers flew
Across the flashing ivory keys
  As if they winked at you.
The music bubbled under
  The magic of her hand
As if the very notes were mad
  To join the festive band.

When Polly struck the measure
  Of two-step or of waltz,
The oldest there grew young again
  And laughed at time's assaults;
While lovely Sweet and Twenty,
  And happy Sweet Sixteen,
Went floating light as thistle-down
  The merry staves between.

When Polly played the lancers
   You should have seen us bow,
And weave the figures out and in;
   Would we were dancing now,
With Polly playing bravely,
   And all the old set there,
Till who'd believe 'twas midnight by
   The clock upon the stair.

Then Polly played as gayly
   As the youngest heart can feel,
And lad and lass we danced amain
   The blithe Virginia reel.
If Cupid sped his arrows,
   Be sure his aim was true,
When Polly played for dancing, and
   The hours fairly flew.

WEDDED HANDS

The year, sweet wife, is on the wane—
    The happy-hearted year,
That brought us only tithes of pain,
    And rounded sheaves of cheer.

Beside the glowing embers we
    Need envy no one's pelf;
Content am I to partner be
    In firm of "Wife and Self."

Swift glide away the last low sands,
    Fast fades the hearth-fire's light;
We face the world with wedded hands—
    Good-night, old year, good-night!

THE AMBULANCE

I NEVER see in our bustling town,
Where the midsummer sun pours fiercely down,
The swift onrush of the ambulance
But I think of the blessed countenance
Of One who walked by lane and field,
And with voice and look the suffering healed.

Still, where the city's woes are thick,
The dear Christ-spirit heals the sick.
And yet he lives in the hearts of men,
And sends his angels with speed again
Wherever the weary plod and fall,
His care and tenderness over all.

And the angels carry lint and lance,
And drive in the city's ambulance;
Are bluff of speech and deft of hand,
And quick with accents of command;
And the wind of their coming clears the way
For a breath of heaven in the darkest day.

THE HOME-BOUND SHIP

FAR out on the stormy ocean
   There's a ship that is faring home,
Cleaving the great green breakers,
   Parting the curd white foam;
Passing the mighty icebergs,
   Crossing the surging sea,
The ship that is bringing my dear ones
   Safely back to me.

Many a ship is sailing
   Forth on the ocean vast;
Laden with gold and spices,
   Gallant from deck to mast;
But only one ship I dream of,
   For only one ship I pray,
The ship that over the ocean
   Is making her home-bound way.

'Tis just as were mine the single
   Home out of all the world,
Just as were mine the only
   Flag to the winds unfurled,
As over the great green billows,
   Parting the curd white foam,
I think of the ship that is hasting,
   Bringing my loved ones home.

A COQUETTE

I am never in doubt of her goodness,
   I am always afraid of her mood,
I am never quite sure of her temper,
   For wilfulness runs in her blood.
She is sweet with the sweetness of spring-
      time—
   A tear and a smile in an hour—
Yet I ask not release from her slightest
   caprice,
   My love with the face of a flower.

My love with the grace of the lily
   That sways on its slender fair stem,
My love with the bloom of the rosebud,
   White pearls in my life's diadem!
You may call her coquette if it please you,
   Enchanting, if shy or if bold,
Is my darling, my winsome wee lassie,
   Whose birthdays are three, when all told.

CAMP ECHOES

"Rally round the flag, boys! Give it to
 the breeze!"
 Bless the dear old fiddle that wakes the
 gallant air.
Once we thundered it in chorus like the
 booming of the seas,
 Wives and sweethearts joining in, with an
 "Amen" to the prayer.

We're a lot of grizzled fellows, not so much
 to look at now!
 Young and full of vigor when the war
 began,
Some behind the counter, and some behind
 the plough,
 But we rallied for the country, enlisted to
 a man.

Counting not the cost, boys! Never sordid
   aims
  Dimmed our record, hasting to the conflict's
     brunt;
Each to serve the nation, we answered to
   our names,
  And the flag before us, we hurried to the
     front.

Can't you see it waving, the banner of our
   love,
  Where the Shenandoah loops and twists
     like mad?
Can't you hear the shouting, the dying
   groans above,
  When we'd won a battle, and—lost the best
     we had?

Blessings on the music of "Tramp, tramp,
   tramp!"
  How it rang its challenge down the serried
     lines,
Cheered us when, like hounds a-leash, we
   strained through days in camp,
  Or crashed, with Sherman's storm-cloud,
     through Georgia's solemn pines.

Here, like useless hulks, boys, we doze the
    days away—
  Doze and dream and spin our yarns; but
    when we come to die,
Lights out, some true hand for us let "taps"
    the last time play,
  Then wrap the flag about us in the bed
    where last we lie.

THE REASON

Something has changed him; yesterday
  He passed me frowning, scarcely bowed,
And almost looked the other way,
  A careless stranger in the crowd.

But now? What grasp of cordial hand!
  What cheery laugh, what genial tone!
'Mid eddying throngs we pause and stand
  As if Broadway were ours alone.

Dear fellow! One word tells the tale;
  'Tis not the world of yesterday;
His heart gives every comrade hail;
  His wife is coming home to-day!

THREE BASKETS

Bertha's basket: Maiden Bertha, with the
    merry dancing eyes,
And the brow whereon a shadow would be
    such a rare surprise—
What has she within this dainty shell of
    rushes silken-lined,
Where so many maiden musings innocently
    are enshrined?

Gayly mingling ends of worsted; beads that
    glitter silver-bright;
Fleece of Shetland, light and airy, lying there
    in waves of white;
Broidered linen, wrought for pastime in the
    dreamy summer hours;
And perhaps a poet's idyl, read amid the
    leaves and flowers.

Bertha's basket: Mother Bertha. Ah, serener
    light hath grown
In the thoughtful eyes; the forehead hath
    some flitting sorrows known.

In the larger basket looking, other handiwork
    we find,
Where the woman's heart its pleasure, love,
    and longing hath enshrined.

Little aprons; little dresses; little trousers
    at the knee
Patched with tender art, that no one shall
    the mother's piecing see;
Flannel, worked with skill and patience; and
    an overflowing store,
Every size, of little stockings, always needing
    one stitch more.

Bertha's basket: Grandma Bertha; for the
    years have run their way,
And it seems in looking backward it was
    only yesterday
That the maiden tripped so lightly, that the
    matron had her cares—
Age slips on so gently, gently, like an angel
    unawares.

Grandma's work is contemplative. With the
    scintillance of steel
Gleam the needles, smooth with flashing off
    the toe or round the heel,

MAIDEN BERTHA

Leisure days have found the lady; but her
    face is deeply lined,
And her heart is as a temple, where are
    hallowed memories shrined.

As along the dusty high-road rise the mile-
    stones one by one,
Telling here and there the distance, until
    all the way is done,
So a woman's basket marks her journey o'er
    the path of life,
Folding dearest work for others, whether she
    be maid or wife.

CONVALESCENT

THE fever went at the turn of the night,
    She lies like a lily white and still,
But her eyes are full of the old love-light;
    She'll live, if it be God's will.

God's will had it been to snatch her away,
    We had bowed, we had knelt, we had
        kissed the rod,
But His own dear will bids our darling stay,
    And we, we just thank God.

HER LETTER

She has written her little letter;
   It was hard enough to do,
With mistress forever ringing the bell
   Always for something new.
When the spelling was very uncertain,
   And the writing's blotted and slow.
But she's written her little letter
   Over the sea to go.

It will carry her last month's wages—
   A couple of pounds at least.
It means for the dear home people
   No end of a happy feast.
A little shawl for her mother,
   And shoes for the baby's feet,
For the pale-faced ailing sister
   Some delicate things to eat.

She follows her little letter
   Over the plunging sea.
She sits again by the smoking peat,
   And leans on her father's knee.

'There are gossiping neighbors calling,
  No end of kith and kin,
And they laugh and chat and linger
  As their endless tales they spin.

And it isn't work forever,
  With bells that make one start;
And it isn't only the wages—
  It's something tugs at the heart
And sets her laughing and crying
  As she follows across the sea
What she wrote at her kitchen-table
  When she had a half-hour free.

BON VOYAGE!

To Eastern lands, far-famed in song and
    story,
  These latest pilgrims turn as to a shrine,
Their faces yearning for the ancient glory
    And fain to catch anew the gleam divine.

In thought their eyes have caught the heav-
    enly vision,
  As his of old who saw the golden stair
Which made his pillowing stone a place
    Elysian,
  While to and fro God's angels journeyed
    there.

Ere many days this world of axe and hammer,
  Of ploughshares cleaving deep a virgin soil,
Will vanish, with its loud, insistent clamor;
  And they, with joy of him who findeth
    spoil,

Will, each in full and overrunning measure,
  Receive the blessing of the early dawn,
Discern the meanings, reap the sheaves of
    pleasure
  The old life keeps, from our swift heart-
    beats gone.

Our share who stay at home will be to capture
A reflex gladness, following day by day
Their happy progress, fancying the rapture
Of dreams come true, along the hallowed way.

For they, by mount and vale and village lowly,
By Jordan's river and Gennesaret's wave,
Will trace the blessed footprints of the Holy,
And live on earth with Him who came to save.

Theirs be the portion of the twelve who clustered
Around the Master, wheresoe'er He went;
Theirs the sweet knowledge of His presence, lustred
By heaven's own light and fulness of content.

Dear friends, our hearts, your company still keeping,
Will overflow in loving prayers for you!
God give you ease and safety, waking, sleeping,
And bring you home—the pilgrim journey through.

SNOWDROP AND CROCUS

Long were the wintry days and cold,
No bloom could pierce the frozen mould,
Chill blew the gale o'er mount and wold.

But who remembers frost and snow,
When sweet to-day the south winds blow,
And birds are flying to and fro?

We hear the robin's flute-note clear;
It is the love-tide of the year;
Soft shadows play on field and mere.

A vestal in her garments white,
The snowdrop gleams in purest light,
The crocus smiles in jewels dight.

Dear April, leading on to May,
Sweet Spring, upon her royal way!
No wonder earth is glad to-day.

VIOLETS

A friend brought sweetest violets,
   And laid them in my lap to-day,
And straight the Winter afternoon
   Put on the brightness of the May.

The silent flowers, with subtle breath,
   Beguiled away my thoughts of pain;
"O heart," their voiceless odor said,
   "Put on thy robes of light again!"

"For Winter wanes, and Spring returns—
   Dear Spring, when all things lovely shine;
And hidden ways and cloistered cells
   Grow radiant as with bloom divine.

"That path cannot be wholly dark
   Which God hath sown with violets:
Lo! on the earth, as in the sky,
   For thee His morning star he sets."

A CLUSTER OF ROSES TO A FRIEND

Roses, beautiful roses,
   Holding the Summer's light,
Each in its graceful carven cup,
   Crimson and yellow and white,
Breathing the sweetest odors,
   Wearing the richest hues,
Distilled from the clouds of heaven,
   And the heaven-ascending dews.

Roses, wonderful roses,
   Their texture royally fine,
Each in its rare completeness
   Wrought by a Hand divine.
The bud with the moss around it,
   The stem with the steadfast brier,
What could so comfort the fainting heart,
   So answer its mute desire?

The roses brought me a blessing,
  For they came in a weary hour,
And sweet were the thoughts they whispered
  Of one, herself a flower.
Ever may bloom about her
  The starriest flowers of the morn,
And still may all her roses
  Be free from the piercing thorn.

But if the thorns must wound her,
  Since oft, in this life of ours,
The sharpest suffering reaches
  Those who have noblest dowers.
May she rest with trust unchanging
  On the strength of the Friend above,
And so shall roses and thorns alike
  Be the gifts of His matchless love.

THE BLOOM OF THE CACTUS

Rare splendor of scarlet in royalest fashion
  My rich flower wears, as it thrills to the shine
Of the proud sun, who loves such a chalice to flash on,
  And pours in its deep heart his nectar divine.

Superbly it greets me, this joyless ascetic,
  So lately whose spiked leaves I fancied to wear
Through slow-waning seasons, a meaning pathetic,
  Upheld like the hands of a martyr in prayer.

Lo! now, for the cross of its standing in duty
  So patient, while near it gay neighbors were bright,
It is suddenly crowned with superlative beauty,
  Transfigured and wondrous in shimmering light.

In shape rare and perfect, in texture like satin,
  In tint like the ruby reflecting the sun,
The flowers around it grow pale and look flat in
  The arrogant shadow of this haughty one.

It is as though, lost, all alone and unmated,
  A beggar maid stood in the court of a king,
Unknown 'mid the throngs who there clamorous waited,
  Till he saw her, and wooed her with robe and with ring.

And throwing the grace of his mantle above her,
  Cried out to the world, "See! this jewel is mine,
I need her, I yearn for her, crown her and love her,"
  So blooms my rich flower in the sun's golden shine.

INFELIX

Who, gazing on thy cradle sleep
  In far sweet days let down from heaven
  (Such days there be to mothers given),
Had thought of shadows gathering deep,

Or caught upon the baby brow
  One faintest sign of furrowing scar,
  One presage of the lurid star
That overarcs thy pathway now.

Not love itself had power to rend
  The future's kind opaque away,
  Not love itself had power to stay
A single dart that fate should send.

Perchance thine angel watching knew,
  And veiled his face, and hushed his song
  One moment in the radiant throng,
Ah, God! what could an angel do,

Seeing in sinister outline
  The portent of that baleful dross
  That sum of grief and shame and loss,
Which only angels could divine?

Yet, even as *infelix* I write,
  A mighty wave blots out the word,
  No human cry but God hath heard!
No dark but melts in heaven's light!

And in great ages yet to be,
  The sorrowful tale forever told,
  Thy God Himself His lost shall fold,
And thine own mother comfort thee.

DAY BY DAY

With staff and shoon I journey,
  Up hill the way I take,
Past many a tangled thicket
  O'ergrown with brier and brake;
And oft my feet are weary,
  And oft my steps are slow,
By day by day I'm nearer
  The land to which I go.

The foes who hate my Master
  Have spread the path with snares,
In hope to stay my progress
  And catch me unawares.
But ever to my spirit
  New light and strength are given,
For never hosts of evil
  Shall bar the road to heaven.

Far worse than all temptations
    That lure me from without
Are grewsome clouds and terrors
    That compass me about.
Dear Lord, Thine eye can measure
    The strife of fears within,
And Thou canst guide me safely,
    Unscathed by shame or sin.

With staff and shoon I journey,
    And still before mine eyes
The Lord who goes before me
    Holds up a radiant prize.
And though I faint and falter
    I yet shall overcome,
And win with saints and angels
    The endless rest at home.

And sweet it is when tired
    Because the way is long,
To pause beside a mile-stone
    And lift a pilgrim's song.
For who shall lose his courage
    However steep the way,
Who, with the Lord to help him,
    Fares onward day by day?

THE OLD SCHOOL-HOUSE

SET on a rounding hill-top
   And weather-stained and gray,
The little mountain school-house
   Looks down on the lonesome way.
No other dwelling is near it,
   'Tis perched up there by itself,
Like an old forgotten chapel
   High on a rocky shelf.

In at the cobwebbed windows
   I peered, and seemed to see
The face of a sweet girl teacher
   Smiling back at me.
There was her desk in the middle,
   With benches grouped anear,
Which fancy peopled with children—
   Grown up this many a year.

Rosy and sturdy children
   Trudging there, rain or shine,
Eager to be in their places
   On the very stroke of nine.

Their dinners packed in baskets—
   Turnover, pie, and cake,
The homely toothsome dainties
   Old-fashioned mothers could make.

Where did the little ones come from?
   Fields green with aftermath
Sleep in the autumn sunshine,
   And a narrow tangled path,
Creeping through brier and brushwood,
   Leads down the familiar way;
But where did the children come from
   To this school of yesterday?

Oh, brown and freckled laddie
   And lass of the apple cheek,
The homes that sent you hither
   Are few and far to seek.
But you climbed these steeps like squirrels
   That leap from bough to bough,
Nor cared for cloud or tempest,
   Nor minded the deep soft snow.

Blithe of heart and of footstep
   You merrily took the road,
Life yet had brought no shadows,
   Care yet had heaped no load.

And safe beneath lowly roof-trees
  You said your prayers at night,
And glad as the birds in the orchard
  Rose up with the morning light.

Gone is the fair young teacher;
  The scholars come no more
With shout and song to greet her,
  As once, at the swinging door.
There are gray-haired men and women
  Who belonged to that childish band,
With troops of their own around them
  In this sunny mountain land.

The old school stands deserted
  Alone on the hill by itself,
Much like an outworn chapel
  That clings to a rocky shelf.
And the sentinel pines around it
  In solemn beauty keep
Their watch, from the flush of the dawning
  Till the grand hills fall asleep.

THE MOTHER'S CHAIR

THE century's day had just begun
  When the bride, as shy as a small gray mouse,
Came home one eve at the set of sun,
  To reign a queen in a wee bit house;
A wee bit house, but love was there,
And its throne was the bride's small rocking-chair.

Time fared along, and the rocking-chair
  Kept pace with the rise and fall of a tune
That the little mother carolled there,
  Slowly and sweetly, rune and croon,
Mother and baby and rockaby,
As the busy and beautiful years flew by.

And the wee bit house was a crowded nest
  That was left one day for a statelier home,
But the small chair stood in its place with the best,
  Throne for the mother, whoe'er might come.
Babies and babies were cradled there
In her tender arms in that rocking-chair.

The years sped on like the waves in a race,
    And small grandchildren fluttered in;
The dear old hearth was the rallying-place
    For a bevy of youthful kith and kin.
Always the centre, standing there
Was the dear little mother's rocking-chair.

Like sifted snowflakes the days trooped on,
    Till the mother heard the angels call;
One sunrise broke with the mother gone—
    Only to heaven—that was all.
But, oh, it was lonely lingering where
We knelt to her in her little chair.

And one of the youngest of all the line,
    A gay girl, just out of college, sits
In that same old chair, and in shade and shine
    A look of her great-grandmother flits
Over her face, so sweet and fair,
As she rests in the prim little rocking-chair.

THE LETTER SHE DID NOT WRITE

It was never set down in black and white,
The loving letter she did not write;
She thought it out as she baked the bread,
As she mended the stockings and made the bed;
She wove its beautiful sentences through
The morning's work that was hers to do;
But it never was written with ink and pen,
For the boys came home from school, and then
She hadn't a chance in black on white
To scribble the letter she did not write.

It never was dropped in the corner box
Which the faithful postman's key unlocks;
It never was even begun, you see,
Though it throbbed with a true heart's constancy;
The far-away mother, the friend beloved,
The kinsman dear, whom it must have moved,

Were touching her hand with tender clasp,
Were holding her heart in insistent grasp,
But it never was sent on its blessed flight,
The dream of a letter she did not write.

She gave up trying the thing at last,
When the busy day was almost past,
Filled with the measure from sun to sun
Of the woman's work which is never done;
The duties sacred which yet seem slight,
The little wrongs which must be set right.
She had found her paper and taken her seat,
When the baby wakened; "Hush, my sweet!"
And Freddie brought her a puzzling sum,
And Teddy deafened her with his drum;
No wonder it faded quite out of sight.
The dear home letter she meant to write.

But yet, ah, yet were the waves of air
Not stirred by her tender, wordless prayer?
And did not her loving heart, full fain,
Send out its cry to her own, and pain
Of longing bring in a subtle way
A pleasure deep in the waning day,
When somehow she felt that an answer bright
Had come to the letter she could not write?

THE UNRETURNING

Earth, knowing not eld, in thy youth all divine,
Though the ages unceasing are evermore thine,
Once more be birth-thrilled, until forth from thy womb
Throng the myriad forms of the world's waking bloom.

For the sweet of the year, great Earth-mother, is here,
And, lo! on the uplands the flowers appear,
And blithe is the wing, and the song it is glad,
And our yearning hearts only are heavy and sad.

Earth, mother undying, thy tender arms keep
So safe in thy bosom the dear things asleep,
So strong is thy pulse-beat to bid them again
Know battle and conquest, and hunger and pain.

The insistence of growth, the fair crown of
 the leaf,
The fruit in its ripeness, the rich bending
 sheaf—
Earth, this thou canst do, yet our dearer
 loves go,
And return not again from their beds hollowed low.

Our hearts are nigh breaking with bliss and
 with dole;
In the midst of the rapture, how lonely the
 soul!
Comes the bird to the green bough, the bud
 to the tree,
But not from the dark come my darlings to
 me.

THANKSGIVING

WHAT time the latest flower hath bloomed,
   The latest bird hath southward flown;
When silence weaves o'er garnered sheaves
   Sweet idyls in our northern zone;
When scattered children rest beside
   The hearth, and hold the mother's hand,
Then rolls Thanksgiving's ample tide
   Of fervent praise across the land.

And though the autumn stillness broods
   Where spring was glad with song and stir,
Though summer's grace leave little trace
   On fields that smiled at sight of her,
Still glows the sunset's altar fire
   With crimson flame and heart of gold,
And faith uplifts, with strong desire
   And deep content, the hymns of old.

We bless our God for wondrous wealth,
   Through all the bright benignant year;
For shower and rain, for ripened grain;
   For gift and guerdon, far and near.

We bless the ceaseless Providence
   That watched us through the peaceful days,
That led us home, or brought us thence,
   And kept us in our various ways.

And if the hand so much that gave
   Hath something taken from our store,
If caught from sight, to heaven's pure light,
   Some precious ones are here no more,
We still adore the Friend above,
   Who, while earth's road grows steep and dim,
Yet comforts us, in tender love,
   And holds our darlings close to Him.

Thanks, then, O God! From sea to sea
   Let every wind the anthem bear!
And hearts be rife through toil and strife,
   With joyful praise and grateful prayer.
Our fathers' God, their children sing
   The grace they sought through storm and sun;
Our harvest tribute here we bring,
   And end it with, "Thy will be done."

Part III

MILE-STONES

CHRISTMAS

We love to think of Bethlehem,
   That little mountain town
To which on earth's first Christmas Day
   Our blessed Lord came down;
A lowly manger for His bed,
   The cattle near in stall,
There, cradled close in Mary's arms,
   He slept, the Lord of all.

If we had been in Bethlehem,
   We too had hasted fain
To see the Babe whose little face
   Knew neither care nor pain.
Like any little child of ours
   He came unto His own,
Though Cross and shame before him stretched
   His pathway to His throne.

If we had dwelt in Bethlehem,
    We would have followed fast,
And where the Star had led our feet
    Have knelt ere dawn was past.
Our gifts, our songs, our prayers had been
    An offering, as He lay,
The Blessed Babe of Bethlehem,
    In Mary's arms that day.

Now breaks the latest Christmas Morn!
    Again the angels sing,
And far and near the children throng
    Their happy hymns to bring.
All heaven is stirred! All earth is glad!
    For down the shining way
The Lord who came to Bethlehem
    Comes yet on Christmas Day.

AUTUMN PLOUGHING

More than the beauty of summer
  Is shed on the hills to-day,
And the fragrant breath of the vintage
  Is borne on the winds away,
As, father and son together,
  The farmers are guiding the plough;
Deep and straight is the furrow
  They set in the green earth now.

"Plough deep," is the old man's counsel,
  As they turn the fallow field
That yet shall laugh with the harvest,
  And wave with a golden yield.
"Plough deep and straight," and the sturdy
  Answer rings back with a will,
As the tilth is ready for sowing
  On the sun-swept reach of hill.

I watch, and over my spirit
  There wafts an echoed psalm,
Sweet as a thought of our Father,
  And full of heaven's balm.

God knows how deep the furrow
    Needed by soul of mine,
Ere the stony soul shall quicken
    And bloom with fruits divine.

And God who cares for the vintage
    When the sap is in the stem,
And God who crowns the summer
    With the autumn's diadem,
And God who all the winter
    Beholds the world's bread grow,
May be trusted for loving kindness
    Though his ploughshare lay me low.

THE CHRISTMAS ANGELS

AGAIN, as of old, the shadows fold, and the
 midnight sky is clear and cold ;
Again, as when the shepherds watched, the
 peasants sleep with their doors unlatched ;
Serene and still over vale and hill, over palace
 gateway and cottage sill,
In snow-white fleece lies the wintry peace,
 and the angels hasten to do God's will.

Ever they keep above our sleep a vigil tender
 and sweet and deep,
But they waken us now, from the skies aglow,
 and the sound of their wings goes to
 and fro.
Hark to the song of that seraph throng,
 who nearest of all to the throne belong.
Hither they come to heart and home, with
 hail to the right that shall smite the
 wrong.

Glory to God! They send abroad harpings
  of heaven on earthly road,
Lifting the Name on their quivering flame,
  as peace and good-will their notes proclaim,
Sending afar without a jar, wherever our
  Father's children are.
The word of grace from the Father's face,
  thrilling in music from star to star.

Sing to us, angels of Christmas, sing, while
  sweet in the day dawn our glad bells
  ring!
Sing of the Love that comes from above,
  brooding and soft as the breast of the
  dove,
While we swift forget the pain and fret, and
  the pitiful things to which life is set,
And leave at the manger all thought of
  danger, and worship the Child, God's
  children yet.

HOLLY AND PINE

When Christmas comes with mirth and cheer
To clasp the circlet of the year,
Then forth we go for holly and pine,
Our wreaths of evergreen to twine;
Then swift we trip across the snow,
To find the gleaming mistletoe,
And straight and tall and branching free,
We haste to choose the Christmas-tree.

When Christmas comes, for Mother and Kate,
All sorts of sweet surprises wait;
And little fingers thrill with joy
As pretty gifts their skill employ.
When Christmas comes each tries her best
To make it beautiful for the rest,
And no one thinks of selfish ease,
But seeks his neighbor to serve and please.

When Christmas comes, there is none so poor
He will turn the beggar from his door;
When Christmas comes the rich and great
Search out their brothers of low estate,
And the sleigh-bells ring, the church-bells chime,
The children sing in the merry time,
And smiles and greetings leap to lips,
That long were set in grief's eclipse,
For angels of comfort come and go,
Within the Yule-Log's radiant glow.

When Christmas comes, I think again,
Heaven stoops to wish good-will to men,
And God, who loves this earth of ours,
With love once more the whole earth dowers;
And the Babe who slept on Mary's knee,
Once more brings peace to you and me;
And storms may beat, and the winds be wild,
But the lowly mother, the Holy Child,
As in the manger, charm us yet.
All strife and evil our souls forget,
And each believing worshipper
Brings gold and frankincense and myrrh,
And the tongues of hate are hushed and dumb,
When again the Christmas angels come.

MISS LUCINDA'S OPINION

BUT why do I keep Thanksgiving?—
　Did I hear you aright, my dear?
Why? When I'm all alone in life,
　Not a chick nor a child to be near;
John's folks all away in the West,
　Lucy across the sea,
And not a soul in the dear old home
　Save a little bound girl and me?

It does look lonesome, I grant it;
　Yet strange as the thing may sound,
I'm seldom in want of company
　The whole of the merry year round—
There's spring when the lilac blossoms,
　And the apple-trees laugh in bloom,
There's summer when great moths flit and
　　glance
　Through the twilight's star-lit gloom.

Then comes the beautiful autumn,
  When every fragrant brier,
Flinging its garlands on fence and wall,
  Is bright as living fire;
And then the white, still winter time,
  When the snow lies warm on the wheat,
And I think of the days that have passed
      away,
  When my life was so young and sweet.

I'm a very happy woman
  To-day, though my hair is white,
For some of my troubles I've overlived,
  And some I keep out of sight.
I'm a busy old woman, you see, dear,
  As I travel along life's road,
I'm always trying as best I can
  To lighten my neighbor's load.

That child? You should think she'd try
      me?
  Does she earn her bread and salt?
You've noticed she's sometimes indolent,
  And indolence is a fault;
Of course it is, but the orphan girl
  Is growing as fast as she can,
And to make her work from dawn till
      dark
  Was never a part of my plan.

I like to see the dimples
   Flash out on the little face,
That was wan enough, and still enough,
   When first she came to the place.
I think she'll do, when she's older;
   A kitten is not a cat,
And now that I look at the thing, my dear,
   I hope she'll never be that.

I'm thankful that life is peaceful;
   I should just be sick of strife,
If, for instance, I had to live along
   Like poor Job Slocum's wife;
I'm thankful I didn't say "yes," my dear,
   thankful as I can be,
When Job, with a sprig in his button-hole,
   Once came a-courting me.

I'm thankful I'm neither poor nor rich,
   Glad that I'm not in debt;
That I owe no money I cannot pay,
   And so have no call to fret.
I'm thankful so many love me,
   And that I've so many to love,
Though my dearest and nearest have gone before
   In the beautiful home above.

I'll always keep Thanksgiving
   In the good, old-fashioned way,
And think of the reasons for gratitude
   In December, and June, and May,
In August, November, and April,
   And the months that come between;
For God is good, and my heart is light,
   And I'd not change place with a queen.

OF ALL DEAR DAYS

Of all dear days is Christmas day
   The dearest and the best;
Still in its dawn the angels sing
   Their song of peace and rest.
And yet the blessed Christ-Child comes
   And walks the shining way,
Which brings to simple earthly homes
   Heaven's light on Christmas day.

Then, deep in silent woods, the trees—
   The hemlock, pine, and fir—
Thrill to the chilly winter breeze,
   And waft a breath of myrrh;

And far and near Kriss Kringle's bells
  Their airy music shake,
And dancing feet of boys and girls
  A sweeter joyance make.

The Christ-Child came to Bethlehem,
  To Mary's happy breast,
And found within her brooding arms
  A warm encircling nest.
And many a tiny cherub child
  In mother's arms to-day
Smiles like the Christ, the undefiled,
  On this dear Christmas day.

The Christ-Child's mother dimly saw
  The cross in faint outline
Above the baby face that held
  Her own in awe divine.
Thus over little cradle-beds
  The sacred passion-flower
Its purple sign of sorrow spreads
  In love's ecstatic hour.

To Mary's feet the Wise Men brought
  Their gifts of gold and spice;
The "Gloria" swept the midnight skies
  To greet her Pearl of Price.

And down the ladder of the stars,
   Across the shining way,
The angels watched the Christ-Child come
   That first dear Christmas day.

Of all dear days is Christmas day
   The very dearest dear,
The crown and clasp and topmost sheaf
   Of all the joyful year.
Then dancing feet of boys and girls
   Go gayly to and fro,
And "Merry, merry Christmas" rings
   In all the winds that blow.

IN BETHLEHEM

Come back to-day to Bethlehem,
  The year is on the wane,
A truce to strife that wearies life,
  A truce to grief and pain,
Oh, heart return to Bethlehem
  And hear its song again!

If siren voices luring thee
  Have turned thy thoughts aside,
If thou hast quaffed the bitter draught
  Of envy or of pride,
If thou in agony of shame
  Hast thy dear Lord denied,

Come back to-day to Bethlehem,
  All in the quickening dawn,
With wistful eyes regard the skies
  Ere yet the gloom is gone.
Oh, list the song of Bethlehem
  Forever pealing on!

Oh, burdened with the weight of sin,
   And worn with many a care,
Here drop thy load, the sunrise road
   Is open at thy prayer.
Return, return to Bethlehem,
   The angels wait thee there!

Come back, come back to Bethlehem!
   Behold the Virgin's Child
By prophets told in ages old,
   The fair, the undefiled!
Lo, peace is born in Bethlehem
   To soothe earth's tumults wild.

Come back to-day to Bethlehem!
   Though thou hast wandered far,
No rest shall fill thy yearning breast
   Until thou see the Star.
Oh, heart return to Bethlehem
   Where yet the angels are!

A CHRISTMAS THOUGHT

The sweetest gift the Father's love
   Sent ever down to men
Came in the stillness and the dark
   That thrilled to music when
All suddenly the hills grew bright
   And flamed athwart the sky
(A rift of heaven across the night)
   The glory from on high.

Strong angels swept their hearts of fire
   And sang of peace to men;
The wondering shepherds heard in awe
   And took their pathway then
Along the hills by crag and steep
   To find the mother-maid,
In whose glad arms that wintry night
   God's gift of gifts was laid.

All heaven was in sweet Mary's heart,
   The Babe had brought it her.
She did not think it strange to see
   The frankincense and myrrh,
The shining gold, the sages gave,
   As poured beneath a throne,
In honor of the kingly one,
   That hour her very own.

So helpless, yet so beautiful,
  Heaven's gift, the undefiled,
Earth's proudest and earth's lowliest
  Bowed down before the Child.
And back to heaven the angels went
  Whose songs had cleft the night,
And Bethlehem's star was lost amid
  The morning's rapturous light.

Heaven's royal gift to earth that day,
  Heaven's gift of life and love,
Was just a helpless little child
  A mother bent above.
Worth more than ransom ever paid,
  In weight of gold or gem,
The child who came to ransom us—
  The Babe of Bethlehem.

And, aye, in many an earthly home
  God's sweetest gift and best
Is still a little child who sleeps
  Upon a mother's breast.
And over every cradled head
  The angels sing to-day,
With something of the sweetness once
  That thrilled the Bethlehem way.

OCTOBER

We are drinking the wine of the ages
  From cups that are brimming over
With the sweet of a honey unbought with
    money,
  Distilled from the heart of the clover.

The fathomless blue of the heaven,
  The beauty and bloom of the day,
Are making us young,—they are waking the
    tongue
  Of the years that have passed away.

'Tis the radiant, rare October,
  With the clusters ripe on the vine,
With scents that mingle in spicy tingle
  On the hill slope's glimmering line.

And summer's a step behind us,
  And autumn's a thought before,
And each fleet, sweet day that we meet on
    the way
  Is an angel at the door.

A THANKSGIVING FEAST

We two are the last my daughter!
   To set the table for two,
Where once we had plates for twenty,
   Is a lonesome thing to do.
But my boys and girls are scattered
   To the east and the west afar,
And one dearer than even the children
   Has passed through the gates ajar.

I'm wanting my bairns for Thanksgiving.
   I thought last night as I lay
Awake in my bed and watching
   For the breaking of the day,
How my heart would leap in gladness
   If a letter should come this morn
To say that they could not leave us here
   To keep the feast forlorn!

Samuel, my son in Dakota,
   Is a rich man, as I hear,
And he'll never let want approach us,
   Save the wanting of him near;

While Jack is in San Francisco,
  And Edward over the sea,
And only my little Jessie
  Is biding at home with me.

And I feel like poor Naomi
  When back to her own she went,
And they said, "Is this Naomi?"
  She well knew what they meant.
I've stayed, and the lads have wandered,
  And the time that was swift to go
When I was brisk and busy
  Is laggard and dull and slow.

O! the happy time for a mother
  Is when her bairns are small,
And into the nursery-beds at night
  She tucks her darlings all;
When the wee ones are about her,
  With gleeful noise and cry,
And she hushes the tumult with a smile,
  Her brood beneath her eye.

But a mother must bear her burden
  When her babes are bearded men,
On 'change and in the army,
  Or scratching away with a pen
In some banker's dusty office,
  As Martin is, no doubt—
A mother must bear her burden,
  And learn to do without.

I know the Scripture teaching,
  To keep the halt and blind,
And the homesick and the desolate,
  At the festal hour in mind.
Of the fat and the sweet a portion
  I'll send to the poor man's door;
But I'm wearying for my children
  To sit at my board once more.

I tell you, Jessie, my darling,
  This living for money and pelf—
It takes the heart from life, dear,
  It robs a man of himself.
This old bleak hill-side hamlet,
  That sends its boys away,
Has a right to claim them back, dear,
  On the fair Thanksgiving day.

Shame on my foolish fretting!
  Here are letters, a perfect sheaf;
Open them quickly, dearest!
  Ah me, 'tis beyond belief!
By ship and train they're hasting,
  Rushing along on the way.
Tell the neighbors all my children
  Will be here Thanksgiving day.

GARDENS

The wide, fair gardens, the rich, lush gardens,
  Which no man planted, and no man tills;
Their strong seeds drifted, their brave bloom
    lifted,
  Near and far over vales and hills;
Sip the bees from their cups of sweetness,
  Poises above them the wild free wing,
And night and morn from their doors are
    borne
  The dreams of the tunes that blithe hearts
    sing.

The waving gardens, the fragrant gardens,
  That toss in the sun by the broad highway,
Growing together, gorse and heather,
  Aster and golden-rod all the day.
Poppies dark with the wine of slumber,
  Daisies bright with the look of dawn,
The gentian blue, and the long year through
  The flowers that carry the seasons on.

The dear old gardens, the pleasant gardens
   Where mother used to potter about,
Tying and pulling, and sparingly culling,
   And watching each bud as its flower
      laughed out;
Hollyhocks here, and the prince's feather,
   Larkspur and primrose, and lilies white,
Sweet were the dear old-fashioned gardens
   Where we kissed the mother and said
      "Good-night."

"The dear old gardens . . .
Where mother used to potter about"

AUTUMN DAYS

INTO the cup of our life to-day
   What sweet, what spice is poured,
When every step of the common way
   Is a garden of the Lord,
With the golden lights and the purple shades
   Blending in rich accord.

As soon might we count the star beams
   Or the sand on the shifting shore,
As number the flowers that baffle
   Desire with more and more,
As if heaven had opened her windows
   And rained them out of her store

By swamp and field and meadow,
   On the edge of the mountain brook,
By the worn old fence and the hedge-row,
   In the tiniest hidden nook—
Flowers in royal splendor
   Wherever you chance to look.

And the zest of the autumn noontide,
   The crisp of the autumn night,
The feeling of rest after labor,
   The wonderful crystal light,
It is joy of joys to be living
   With the year at its crowning height.

Thank God for the beauty broadcast
   Over our own dear land;
Thank God, who, to feed His children,
   Opens His bounteous hand;
Thank God for the lavish harvests,
   Thank Him from strand to strand.

THE LOVING-CUP

'Tis the time of year for the loving-cup
   To pass from hand to hand,
When the sounds of wassail and revelry
   Are echoing o'er the land.
For North, where the skater skims the mere,
   And South, where the redbird sings,
A pulse of cheer to the waning year
   The merry Christmas brings.

'Tis the time of the year for the open hand
   And the tender heart and true,
When a rift of Heaven has cleft the skies,
   And the saints are looking through.
The flame leaps high where the hearth was drear,
   And sorrowful eyes grow bright,
For a message dear that all may hear
   Is borne on the Christmas light.

'Tis the time of year for the cordial word
   And the grace of the lifted load,
For brother to come to brother's help
   On the rough and stony road.
'Tis the time to bury the ancient grudge,
   And to make the quarrels up;
No hate has room where the roses bloom
   'Round the Christmas loving-cup.

'Tis the time of year for children's joy,
   And all in a scarlet row
The stockings hang in the ingle nook,
   And the dreaming faces glow.
And the children turn and laugh in sleep,
   To-morrow will be so gay;
For there never is mirth in this queer old earth,
   Like the mirth of Christmas day.

'Tis the time of year for the loving-cup,
   When the holly berries shine,
And with shout and song of man and maid,
   The cedar and fir we twine.
Ah! pass the cup from the frozen North
   To the South, where the robin sings,
For a pulse of cheer to the waning year
   The merry Christmas brings.

'Tis the time of year for the sweet surprise,
  For the blessing we did not see,
Though straight from the infinite love of God
  'Twas coming to you and me.
'Tis the time for seeking once again
  The sheen of the Bethlehem star;
And for kneeling fain, with the age-long train,
  Where the Babe and Mary are.

THE DAYS WHEN NOTHING HAPPENS

For the days when nothing happens,
    For the cares that leave no trace,
For the love of little children,
    For each sunny dwelling-place,
For the altars of our fathers,
    And the closets where we pray,
Take, O gracious God and Father,
    Praises this Thanksgiving day.

For our harvests safe ingathered,
    For our golden store of wheat,
For the cornlands and the vinelands,
    For the flowers up-springing sweet,
For our coasts from want protected,
    For each inlet, river, bay,
By Thy bounty full and flowing,
    Take our praise this joyful day.

For the dangers to the Nation
    Warded hence by sovereign love,
For the country, strong and hopeful,
    Songs arise to God above.

Never people called and chosen
  Had such loving-kindness shown
As this people, God-defended!
  Therefore, praises to the throne!

For our dear ones lifted higher
  Through the darkness to the light,
Ours to love and ours to cherish
  In dear memory, beyond sight,
For our kindred and acquaintance
  In Thy heaven who safely stay,
We uplift our psalms of triumph,
  Lord, on this Thanksgiving day.

For the quiet, uneventful,
  Blessed progress of our lives,
For the love of friends and neighbors,
  Parents, children, husbands, wives,
For the ever-present knowledge
  That our Saviour is our own,
On this day of glad Thanksgiving
  Praises rise to reach the throne.

For the hours when heaven is nearest
  And the earth-mood does not cling,
For the very gloom oft broken
  By our looking for the King,
By our thought that He is coming,
  For our courage on the way,
Take, O Friend, unseen, eternal,
  Praises this Thanksgiving day.

GOOD-NIGHT

Good-night, sweet year, that brought to me
  Dear friends to love, rare wealth to hold,
That gave me flowers for memory
  More precious far than fleeting gold.
Good-night, sweet year, wherein I read
  Full many a page with rare delight;
Thy latest hour will soon have fled
  Oh, pleasant year, sweet year, good-night!

Good-night, sad year, that reft away
  Some hopes I cherished; gave the pain
Of disillusion; dimmed the day
  With wrecks of labor wrought in vain.
Good-night, sad year, that sometime knew
  My pillow wet with bitter tears,
Good-night, sad year, that drifteth too
  Far hence on Time's black sea of years.

Good-night, blithe year, that to the home
   Came smiling with so gay a face,
Bade roses bloom in hall and room,
   Sent small feet pattering through the place,
That woke such bells of melody
   As touch the eternal chords that ring
Where evermore the ransomed be
   And saints for aye behold the King.

Good-night, brave year, that gave me strength,
   And helped my will to overcome
In struggles, where the foe, at length
   Baffled and beaten, left me dumb,
Yet thrilling with victorious song!
   Good-night, brave year! I fain would keep
Thy secret still to right the wrong,
   But thou art weary. Rest and sleep.

Good-night, O year, most sorrowful
   Seen from the earth side, ache and loss
And clouded dawns, and dear ones gone,
   Have deeply stamped thee with the cross.
Good-night, O sorrowful, sweet year,
   Sweet with the promise of the day,
Where heaven's own morning shall appear
   And all the shadows flee away.

THE NEW YEAR

The clock struck twelve in the tall church
    tower,
  And the old year slipped away,
To be lost in the crowd of phantom years
    In the House of Dreams that stay
      All wrapped in their cloaks of gray.

Then swift and sweet o'er the door's worn
    sill
  Came the youngest child of Time,
With a gay little bow and a merry laugh,
    And a voice like bells achime,
      Challenging frost and rime.

He found there was plenty for him to do,
  The strong and the weak were here,
And both held out their hands to him
    And gave him greetings dear,
      The beautiful young new year.

"You must bring us better days," they said,
  "The old year was a cheat."
Which I think was mean when the year
    was dead;
  Such fate do dead years meet,
    To be spurned by scornful feet!

"I bring you the best a year can bring,"
  The new-comer stoutly spake,
"The chance of work, the gift of trust,
  And the bread of love to break,
    If but my gifts you'll take!"

The noblest thing a year can lay
  In the lap of you or me,
The brave new year has brought this day—
  It is Opportunity,
    Which the wise are swift to see.

AT THE PARTING OF THE WAYS

"Go forth in thy turn," said the Lord of
    the years to the year we greet to-day—
"Go forth to succor my people, who are
    thronging the world's highway.

"Carry them health and comfort, carry them
    joy and light,
The grace of the eager dawning, the ease
    of the restful night.

"Take them the flying snowflake, and the
    hope of the hastening spring,
The green of the leaf unrolling, the gleam
    of the bluebird's wing.

"Give them the gladness of children, the
    strength of sinew and nerve,
The pluck of the man in battle, who may
    fall, but will never swerve.

"Send them the lilt of the singer, the sword
    that is swift to smite
In the headlong rush of the onset, when the
    wrong resists the right.

"Pour on them peace that crowneth hosts
    which have bravely striven,
Over them throw the mantle they wear who
    are God-forgiven.

"Shrive them of sin and of blunders; oh,
    make my people free!
Let this year among years be thought of as
    a time of jubilee,

"Throbbing with notes triumphant, waving
    with banners fair,
A year of the grace of the Highest, to
    vanquish human despair.

"For sorrow and sighing send them, O Year,
    the dance of mirth,
And banish the moan and the crying from
    the struggling, orphaned earth.

"Go forth in thy turn, O blithe New Year,"
    said the Lord of the passing days;
And the angels in heaven heard Him, and
    lifted a pæan of praise.

THE THINNING RANKS

The day grows lonelier; the air
  Is chillier than it used to be.
We hear about us everywhere
  The haunting chords of memory.
Dear faces once that made our joy
  Have vanished from the sweet home band,
Dear tasks that were our loved employ
  Have dropped from out our loosened hand.

Familiar names in childhood given
None call us by, save those in heaven.
We cannot talk with later friends
Of those old times to which love lends
Such mystic haze of soft regret;
We would not, if we could, forget
The sweetness of the by-gone hours,
So priceless are love's faded flowers;

But lonelier grows the waning day,
And much we miss upon the way
Our comrades who have heard the call
That soon or late must summon all.

Ah, well! the day grows lonelier *here*.
Thank God, it doth not yet appear
What thrill of perfect bliss awaits
Those who pass on within the gates.
Oh, dear ones who have left my side,
And passed beyond the swelling tide,
I know that you will meet me when
I, too, shall leave these ranks of men
And find the glorious company
Of saints from sin forever free,
Of angels who do always see
The face of Christ, and ever stand
Serene and strong at God's right hand.

The day grows lonelier, the air
   Hath waftings strangely keen and cold,
But woven in, O glad, O rare,
   What love-notes from the hills of gold!
Dear crowding faces gathered there,
   Dear blessed tasks that wait our hand,
What joy, what pleasure shall we share,
   Safe anchored in the one home-land.

Close up, O comrades, close the ranks,
   Press onward, waste no fleeting hour!
Beyond the outworks, lo! the banks
   Of that full tide, where life hath power,
And Satan lieth underfoot,
And sin is killed, even at the root.
Close up, close fast the wavering line,
Ye who are led by One divine.
The day grows lonelier apace,
But heaven shall be our trysting-place.

Part IV

CLOSET AND ALTAR

JESUS WENT BEFORE

Their faces to Jerusalem,
  They stepped with laggard feet,
Half timorous, defiant half,
  At what they went to meet.
But as they rested, or they talked
  Their sad forebodings o'er,
Still leading on the little band,
  Their Master went before.

He saw in vision maddened throngs;
  He saw the crowded hall
Where scribe and priest should mock and flout,
  Where cruel scourge should fall;
He saw the cross; its shadows lay
  The toilsome pathway o'er;
But, pressing on with ardent soul,
  The Master went before.

To-day Thy pledged disciples, Lord,
  Meet sorrow, pain, and shame,
Their watchword in the trial time
  Thine own all-conquering name.
Though flesh be weak, and spirit faint,
  And heart be spent and sore,
They cannot fail in any strife
  While Thou shalt go before.

In presence of Thy bitter foes,
   In midst of dark defeat,
They yet shall snatch a victory
   And taste a triumph sweet;
Nor death itself shall crush them, Lord.
   Its final conflict o'er,
The ransomed hosts shall shout and sing,
   "Our Master went before!"

NOT READY

Out of our pain and struggle,
   Up from our grief and dole,
We are swift to cry to the Healer
   For the touch that makes us whole.

Alas! we are not so ready,
   In the day of our joy and crown,
With the palms and the fragrant incense
   Laid at His altar down.

And how it must grieve the Master
   That His own are so slow to praise,
In the flush of their peace and gladness,
   The goodness which brims the days!

JOINT HEIRS

THERE came a precious meaning
   Into the Word to-day—
A waft of sweetness from the land
   That is not far away,
A thought so pure, so high, so strong,
   That in my lonely lot
I kept the measure of a song,
   A song where pain is not.

Joint heirs with Christ the Blessed,
   The Father's equal Son,
So lifted into equal place
   With that beloved One,
So given rights of sonship
   Before the Father's face,
So made the heir of all things,
   By Heaven's most royal grace.

Not as the younger children
   Who forth from home may fare,
But as the first-born of the line
   The birthright I shall share.

In the presence of the Father,
   Uplifted by the Son,
I shall be loved as Christ is loved,
   And dwell anear His throne.

Dear thought that bids me cherish
   To-day the hidden name
Which will be mine when Jesus
   His own shall come to claim;
Dear hope that casts its glory,
   A charm o'er daily care,
And gives me joy and freedom
   Oft as I kneel in prayer.

Joint heir with Christ the Blessed,
   The Christ-life mine to live,
And every day some sacrifice
   Of mine own will to give:
Some trial to endure for Him,
   Some brother's load to ease,
Or in the quiet home routine
   Some little child to please.

Joint heir with Christ in heaven,
   Joint heir with Christ on earth,
Made equal in the Father's sight,
   Divinely dowered in birth.
A waft of precious meaning
   Comes floating from that word,
A harp note from the ceaseless strain
   By saints and angels heard.

THE DEAREST ONE

OH! which of all my dearest dear is most my very own?
Whom do I pray for oftenest when kneeling at the throne?
'Tis not the one whose earthly cup is brimmed with gift and grace,
Nor yet the one whose winsome heart looks from the bonniest face;
The dearest dear of all mine own is one in greatest need,
The one whose burden heaviest weighs, whose path is rough indeed.
For him I claim the help of Heaven, for him I cling about
The cross of the All-pitiful till flesh and strength give out;
And still it is the neediest for whom I plead and pray,
What time I bring my dearest dear to Christ at fall of day.

If, all imperfect as I am, thus love doth reign in me,
How better far, and truer far, must Christ the shepherd be,
Whose greater love hath largesse for the weakest of his own—
Who, by the hunger and the thirst, the faintness and the moan,
Doth measure still the bounty that, outflowing day by day,
Uplifts and helps the weary one who stumbleth in the way.
Dear Love, sweet Love, thy dearest dear, 'tis he who most hath need,
Whose want and weakness are his prayer, and without word can plead.

A SONG OF THE BURDEN BEARER

Over the narrow footpath
  That led from my lowly door,
I went with a thought of the Master,
  As oft I had walked before;
My heart was heavily laden,
  And with tears my eyes were dim,
But I knew I should lose the burden
  Could I get a glimpse of Him.

Over the trodden pathway,
  Through the fields all shorn and bare,
I went with a step that faltered,
  And a face that told of care;
I had lost the light of the morning,
  With its shimmer of sun and dew,
But a gracious look of the Master
  Would the strength of morn renew.

While yet my courage wavered,
   And the sky before me blurred,
I heard a voice behind me
   Saying a tender word;
And I turned to see the brightness
   Of heaven upon the road,
And suddenly lost the pressure
   Of the weary, crushing load.

Nothing that hour was altered,
   I had still the weight of care,
But I bore it now with the gladness
   Which comes of answered prayer;
No grief the soul can fetter
   Nor cloud its vision, when
The dear Lord gives the spirit
   To breathe to His will, Amen.

VESPERS

I leave the city behind me,
   Shaking its dust from my feet;
Leaving its thunder and roar of trade,
   I haste to the covert sweet,
Where from the elm-boughs arching,
   As in long cathedrals dim,
Through the hush of the lingering twilight
   The thrushes sing a hymn.

In the town were hurry and bustle,
   And squalor and sin were there,
And the trail of the worship of Mammon,
   And the burden of strenuous care.
In the fields are silence and perfume,
   And one may kneel and pray
In the calm and cloistered forest
   At the tender fall of day.
The birds go flying homeward
   To the nest in the tree-tops dim,
And the vespers die into stillness—
   The thrush has finished his hymn.

Oh, beautiful lanes, I love you
   As you skirt the babbling brooks,
As you seek the foot of the mountain,
   As you find the hidden nooks,
Where the ferns in great green masses
   The edge of the swamp-land rim,
Where I linger till stars awake above
   And the thrushes sing their hymn.

"In the fields are silence and perfume"

ONE STEP AT A TIME

There's a mine of comfort for you and me
　In a homely bit of truth
We were tenderly taught, at the mother's knee,
　In the happy days of youth.
It is, what though the road be long and steep,
　And we too weak to climb,
Or, what though the darkness gather deep,
　We take one step at a time.

A single step and again a step,
　Until, by safe degrees,
The mile-stones past, we win at last
　Home when the King shall please.
And the strangest thing is often this:
　That the briery, tangled spots
Which cumber our feet are thick and sweet
　With our Lord's forget-me-nots.

It matters little the pace we take
　　If we journey sturdily on,
With the burden bearer's steady gait,
　　Till the day's last hour is gone,
Or if with the dancing foot of the child,
　　Or the halting step of age,
We keep the goal in the eye of the soul
　　Through the years of our pilgrimage.

And yet in the tramp of appointed days
　　This thing must sometimes be,
That we falter and pause and bewildered
　　　gaze,
　　For the road has led to the sea.
And the foeman's tread is on our track,
　　As once on the booming coast
Where the children of Israel, looking back,
　　Saw Pharaoh's threatening host.

Then clear from the skies our Leader's voice,
　　"Go forward," bids us dare
Whatever we meet with fearless feet
　　And the might of trustful prayer.
So, ever advancing day by day,
　　In the Master's strength sublime,
Even the lame shall take the prey,
　　Marching a step at a time.

And what of the hours when hand and foot
  We are bound and laid aside,
With the fevered vein, and the throbbing pain,
  And the world at its low ebb-tide?
And what of our day of the broken heart,
  When all that our eyes can see
Is the vacant space, where the vanished face
  Of our darling used to be?

Then, waiting and watching, and almost spent,
  Comes peace from the Lord's own hand,
In His blessed will, if we rest content,
  Though we cannot understand.
And we gather anew our courage and hope
  For the road so rough to climb;—
With trial and peril we well may cope,
  A single step at a time.

THE WORD SHE REMEMBERED

"You remember the sermon you heard, my
    dear?"
  The little one blushed and dropped her
    eyes,
Then lifted them bravely, with look of
    cheer—
  Eyes that were blue as the summer skies.

"I'm afraid I forgot what the minister said,
  He said so much to grown-up men,
And the pulpit was 'way up over my head;
  But I told mamma that he said 'Amen.'

"And 'Amen,' you know, means 'Let it
    be,'
  Whatever our Lord may please to do,
And that is sermon enough for me,
  If I mind and feel so, the whole week
    through."

I took the little one's word to heart,
  I wish I could carry it all day long,
The "Amen" spirit, which hides the art
  To meet each cross with a happy song.

TE DEUM LAUDAMUS

We praise Thee! We bless Thee!
  O Saviour, risen to-day!
Thou who didst drain the bitter cup
Thou who Thy life didst offer up,
  To take our sins away!

We praise Thee! We bless Thee!
  O Lord of death and life!
We follow where Thy feet have gone,
Through deepest night to fairest dawn,
  To peace through stubborn strife!

We praise Thee! We bless Thee!
  Even when our hearts are riven!
Thou art anear the dying bed,
Thy hand beneath the fainting head,
  And Thou Thyself art heaven!

We praise Thee! We bless Thee!
   Beside each lowly mound
That, daisy-starred or lily-sown,
Is but the cover gently thrown
   O'er one in Jesus found.

We praise Thee! We bless Thee!
   With every pulse and breath.
Ours is the never-ending hymn
That saints began in ages dim,
   Thou Conqueror of Death!

We praise Thee! We bless Thee!
   This happy Sabbath day.
Through earth and skies the chorus rings,
O Lord of lords and King of kings,
   Who takes our sins away.

THINE IS THE POWER

Thine is the power, Lord,
　Ours is the need;
Trusting Thy precious word,
　Dare we to plead.
Weaker than infants are,
　Lonely and sad,
Thou art our Morning Star:
　Oh, make us glad.

Thine is the power, Lord,
　Empty are we;
All grace with Thee is stored,
　Filled let us be.
Vessels Thy hand has made,
　Use us, we pray;
So be Thy love displayed
　In us each day.

Thine is the power, Lord,
　Thou wilt provide;
Thou canst the strength afford,
　When we are tried;
Sorrows around us meet,
　Deep the dark wave,
Still is Thy promise sweet,
　Yet Thou wilt save.

Thine is the power, Lord,
　　Therefore we come,
Trusting Thy precious word,
　　Thou art our home.
Till in Thine arms we rest,
　　Homesick are we;
Fold us to Thy dear breast,
　　Draw us to Thee.

A THOUGHT

Seen by memory's magic,
　　Yesterday is golden;
Hope illumes the morrow;
　　Eyes are only holden
From some fair illusion
　　When they view to-day,
With its mists of morning,
　　Bitter blown away.

Yet of all the morrows
　　That from me are hidden;
All the bright days ended
　　Coming back unbidden;
None or was or will be
　　Richer in its way
Than this open-handed,
　　Slightly prized to-day.

FOLDED HANDS

PALE, withered hands that more than four-
 score years
Had wrought for others — soothed the hurt
 of tears,
Rocked children's cradles, eased the fever's
 smart,
Dropped tenderest balm in many an aching
 heart—
Now stirless folded, like wan rose-leaves
 pressed
Above the snow and silence of her breast.
In mute appeal they tell of labors done
And well-earned rest that came with set of
 sun;
From the worn brow the lines of care are
 swept
As if an angel's kiss the while she slept
Had smoothed the cobweb wrinkles quite
 away
And given back the peace of childhood's
 day.

A smile is on the lips as if she said,
"None know life's secret save the happy dead."
And, gazing where she lies, we feel that pain
And parting cannot cleave her soul again.
And we are sure that they who saw her last
In that dim vista which we call the past,
Who never knew her old and weary-eyed,
Remembering best the maiden and the bride,
Have sprung to greet her with the olden speech,
The dear sweet names no later love can teach,
And "Welcome Home" they cried, and grasped her hands—
So dwells the mother in the best of lands.

THE CURTAIN FALLS

Over the sorrow and over the bliss,
Over the tear-drop, over the kiss,
Over the crimes that blotted and blurred,
Over the wound of the hasty word,
Over the deeds in weakness done,
Over the battles lost and won,
Now at the end of the flying year,
Year that to-morrow will not be here,
Over our freedom, over our thralls,
In the hush of the midnight the curtain falls.

Over our gain and over our loss,
Over our crown and over our cross,
Over the fret of our discontent,
Over the ill that we never meant,
Over the scars of our self-denial,
Over the strength that conquered trial,
Now in the end of the flying year,
Year that to-morrow will not be here,
Quietly final, the prompter calls;
Swiftly the dusk of the curtain falls.

Over the crowds and the solitudes,
Over our shifting, hurrying moods,
Over the hearths where bright flames leap
Over the cribs where the babies sleep,
Over the clamor, over the strife,
Over the pageantry of life,
Now in the end of the flying year,
Year that to-morrow will not be here,
Swiftly and surely, from starry walls,
Silently downward the curtain falls.

THE END

www.ingramcontent.com/pod-product-compliance
Lightning Source LLC
Chambersburg PA
CBHW030302170426
43202CB00009B/840